SOUTH CAROLINA

Anita Yasuda

www.av2books.com

AV² provides enriched content that supplements and complements this book. Weigl's AV² books strive to create inspired learning and engage young minds in a total learning experience.

Your AV² Media Enhanced books come alive with...

 Audio
Listen to sections of the book read aloud.

 Video
Watch informative video clips.

 Embedded Weblinks
Gain additional information for research.

 Try This!
Complete activities and hands-on experiments.

 Key Words
Study vocabulary, and complete a matching word activity.

 Quizzes
Test your knowledge.

 Slide Show
View images and captions, and prepare a presentation.

... and much, much more!

Go to **www.av2books.com**, and enter this book's unique code.

BOOK CODE

D 8 2 6 8 5 2

AV² by Weigl brings you media enhanced books that support active learning.

Published by AV² by Weigl
350 5th Avenue, 59th Floor
New York, NY 10118
Website: www.av2books.com   www.weigl.com

Library of Congress Cataloging-in-Publication Data

Yasuda, Anita.
 South Carolina : the Palmetto State / Anita Yasuda.
   p. cm. -- (Explore the U.S.A.)
 Includes bibliographical references and index.
 ISBN 978-1-61913-401-0 (hard cover : alk. paper) -- ISBN 978-1-61913-402-7 (soft cover : alk. paper)
 1. South Carolina--Juvenile literature. I. Title.
 F269.3.Y27 2013
 975.7--dc23
                                        2012016260

ISBN 978-1-61913-401-0 (hard cover)

Printed in the United States of America in North Mankato, Minnesota
1 2 3 4 5 6 7 8 9 16 15 14 13 12

Project Coordinator: Karen Durrie
Art Director: Terry Paulhus

Weigl acknowledges Getty Images as the primary image supplier for this title.

SOUTH CAROLINA

Contents

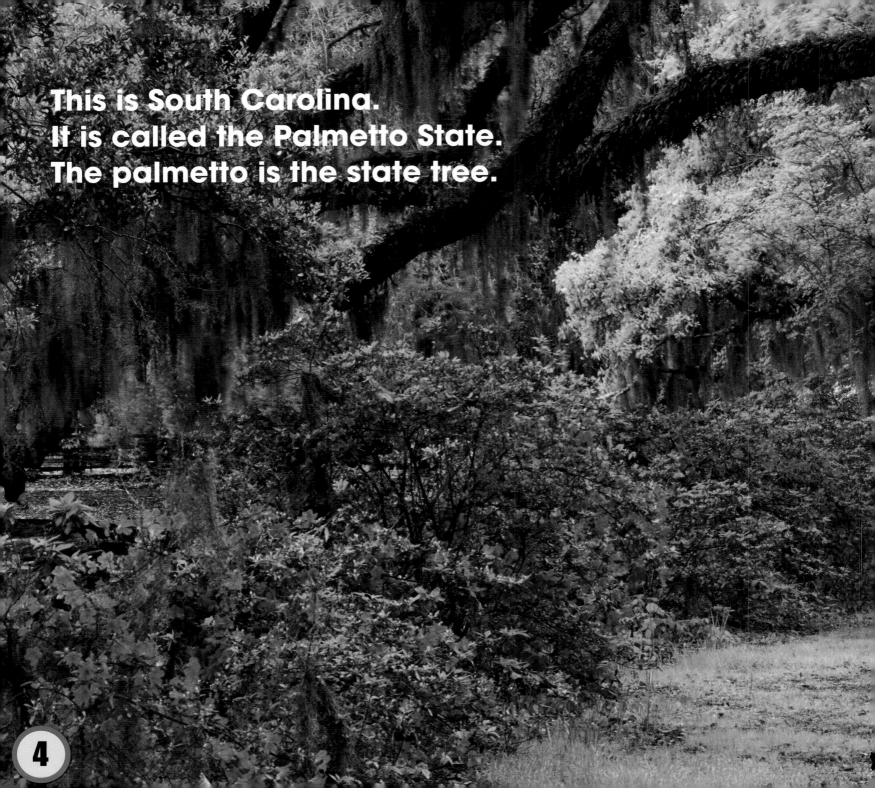

This is South Carolina.
It is called the Palmetto State.
The palmetto is the state tree.

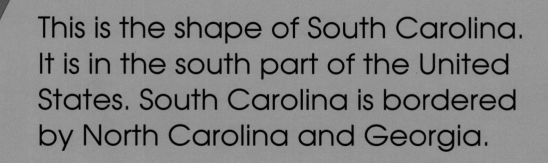

This is the shape of South Carolina. It is in the south part of the United States. South Carolina is bordered by North Carolina and Georgia.

Where is South Carolina?

Canada

United States

Pacific Ocean

Atlantic Ocean

Mexico

South Carolina is next to the Atlantic Ocean.

People from England came to live in South Carolina about 400 years ago. Some people owned large farms called plantations. They grew rice and cotton.

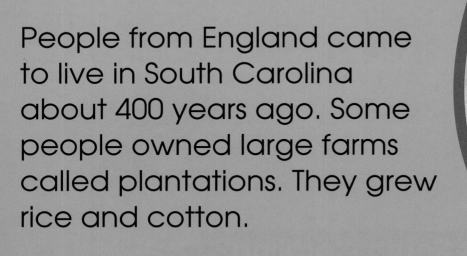

There are still plantations in parts of South Carolina.

The yellow jessamine is the South Carolina state flower. It grows up trees and along fences.

The South Carolina state seal has a tree, a goddess, and branches.

The goddess stands for hope.

This is the state flag of South Carolina. It has a crescent and a palmetto tree on it.

The South Carolina flag is blue and white.

843-318-9010

13

The state bird of South Carolina is the Carolina wren. This small bird lives in forests, swamps, and near farms.

Carolina wrens often live in pairs.

This is the biggest city in South Carolina. It is named Columbia. Columbia is the state capital.

Seibels House is believed to be the oldest building in Columbia. It is 200 years old.

Forests cover much of South Carolina. Wood from South Carolina is used all over the world.

Southern yellow pine is often used to make homes.

South Carolina is known
for its mountains, beaches,
and museums.

People come to hike, swim,
and see historic places.

SOUTH CAROLINA FACTS

These pages provide detailed information that expands on the interesting facts found in the book. These pages are intended to be used by adults as a learning support to help young readers round out their knowledge of each state in the *Explore the U.S.A.* series.

Pages 4–5

South Carolina has a warm climate. The palmetto tree grows well in the subtropical forests of the state. It grows along the state's coast. The palmetto tree has an important place in South Carolina's history. It represents the defense of the palmetto-log fort by Colonel William Moultrie and his troops during the American Revolution.

Pages 6–7

On May 23, 1788, South Carolina became the eighth state to join the United States. South Carolina is one of the original 13 colonies that formed the country. South Carolina is bordered by North Carolina to the north and northeast, Georgia to the west and southwest, and the Atlantic Ocean to the east and southeast.

Pages 8–9

On December 20, 1860, South Carolina became the first state to separate from the United States. During the Civil War, it joined the Confederate States of America. The coast of South Carolina was the site of much fighting during the war. South Carolina rejoined the United States in 1868, three years after the Confederacy was defeated.

Pages 10–11

In 1924, the yellow jessamine became the official flower of South Carolina. Many flowers, including roses and irises, grow in the state. The state seal is made up of two ovals. The palmetto tree is on the left, and the goddess of hope is on the right. The goddess is shown walking over discarded weapons. Above her is the state motto, "While I breathe, I hope."

Pages 12–13

On January 28, 1861, the South Carolina flag became official. The flag's blue color matched the uniform color of South Carolina's American Revolution troops. The flag's crescent represents the silver emblem worn on the soldiers' caps. The palmetto tree on the flag represents the defense of the palmetto-log fort on Sullivan's Island.

Pages 14–15

Carolina wrens mate for life. They do not migrate. Instead, they live in one territory year-round. They build nests with an assortment of materials including pine needles, leaves, and dried grasses. Carolina wrens are known for their songs. These songs are loud and high-pitched.

Pages 16–17

Columbia became the capital in 1786 because of its central location within the state. More than 130,000 people live in Columbia. While two-thirds of Columbia burned to the ground during the Civil War, the city still has many historic buildings. This includes the First Baptist Church, where South Carolinians decided to leave the United States.

Pages 18–19

Two-thirds of South Carolina are covered in forests. Today, forestry is one of the top industries in South Carolina. Each year, timber generates $17 billion to South Carolina's economy. The forestry industry employs about 45,000 people. South Carolina exports $1.3 billion in forest products each year.

Pages 20–21

South Carolina's coastline covers 187 miles (300 kilometers). The state has well-known beaches such as Myrtle Beach. Visitors come to South Carolina to explore nature and see the many historic sites. They travel to Charleston to tour colonial-era buildings and places such as Fort Sumter, the site of the first Civil War battle.

KEY WORDS

Research has shown that as much as 65 percent of all written material published in English is made up of 300 words. These 300 words cannot be taught using pictures or learned by sounding them out. They must be recognized by sight. This book contains 54 common sight words to help young readers improve their reading fluency and comprehension. This book also teaches young readers several important content words, such as proper nouns. These words are paired with pictures to aid in learning and improve understanding.

Page	Sight Words First Appearance
4	is, it, state, the, this, tree
7	and, by, in, next, of, part, to, where
8	about, are, came, farms, from, large, live, people, some, still, there, they, years
11	a, along, for, grows, has, up
12	on, white
15	near, often, small
16	be, city, named, old
19	all, homes, make, much, over, used, world
21	come, its, mountains, places, see

Page	Content Words First Appearance
4	palmetto, South Carolina
7	Atlantic Ocean, Georgia, North Carolina, shape, United States
8	cotton, England, plantations, rice
11	branches, fences, flower, goddess, hope, seal, yellow jessamine
12	crescent, flag
15	bird, Carolina wren, forests, pairs, swamps
16	building, capital, Columbia, Seibels House
19	southern yellow pine, wood
21	beaches, museums